Graphics Processing Units,
an overview

Patrick H. Stakem
(c) 2017, 2022

Number 16 in the
Computer Architecture Series

Introduction

This book discusses the topic of Graphics Processing Units, which are specialized units found in most modern computer architectures. Although we can do operations on graphics data in regular arithmetic logic units (ALU's) via software, the hardware approach is much faster. Just like for floating point arithmetic, specialized units speed up the process. We will discuss the applications for GPU's, the data format, and the operations they perform. These specialized units are the backbone to video, and to a large extent, audio processing in modern computer architectures.

The assumption is made that your understand basically the difference between integers, floating point, and graphics objects, and you have an understanding of how a computer executes instructions. A basic knowledge of memory and caching will be useful.

The GPU is a specialized computer architecture, focused on image data manipulation for graphics displays and picture processing. It has specific applications for that. The normal ALU, Arithmetic-Logic Unit, in a computer does the four basic math operations, and logical operations on integers. These integers are usually 32 or 64 bits at this time. The GPU greatly enhances the speed of 3D graphics.

GPU's find application in arcade machines, games consoles, pc's, tablets, phones, car dashboards, tv's and entertainment systems. Most of the World's top Supercomputers are based on massive numbers of GPU's. This is leading to the interesting concept of Cloud-based supercomputing, and the quite real prospect of personal supercomputing.

First, we'll look at the CPU, and the operations it performs on data. The CPU is fairly flexible on what it does, because of software. You can implement a GPU in software, but it won't be very fast. There's a similar co-processor, the floating point unit (FPU) that operates on specially formatted data. You can implement the floating point unit in software, actually, you can probably download the library, but it won't be as fast as using a dedicated piece of hardware. We'll first discuss integer data format, and operations on those data. The "L" part of ALU says we can also do logical operations on data.

GPU's can process integer and floating point data much faster than a cpu, if it is presented in the right format. They don't have all the general purpose features of ALU's, but they can contain 100 cores or more. This has lead to the employment of large numbers of GPU's as the basis for the current generation of Supercomputers.

Author

Mr. Patrick H. Stakem received a Bachelors degree in Electrical Engineering from Carnegie-Mellon University, and Masters Degrees in Physics and Computer Science from the Johns Hopkins University.

He has taught for the Graduate Computer Science program at Loyola University in Maryland, and for Capitol Technology University.

Mr. Stakem was affiliated with the the Whiting School of Engineering of the Johns Hopkins University, Loyola University of Maryland, and the Capitol Institute of Technology.

Mr. Stakem can be found of Facebook and Linkedin.

Integer data format

If we take a grouping of bits and treat it like a positional, signed number, we have an integer. Integers have a finite range. Eight bits gives us 256 (2^8) numbers, and 16 bits gives us nearly 65000. We need to give up one bit (or, 1/2 of our range of numbers) for a sign position. Integers are mostly 32- or 64-bits wide.

Computer circuitry doesn't do math, it does logical operations on data. Luckily, the math operations can be expressed in term of logical operations. This is just a quirk of the basis technology. The other problem is, we tend to do our math in base 10, only because we have 10 toes. Computers do their math in terms of base 2, because the switching and storage elements have 2 states. For microelectronics, the base-2 is used, because the physics of the devices allow for representation and recognition of two different states easily and efficiently. We do agree, however, on a positional notation, which allows us to use digit positions to represent different orders of magnitude. This makes most operations easy, as compared to doing long division in Roman numerals, a non-positional system.

We also need to consider the important concept of zero, which was used in early Mesoamerica, China, India, and other places. The Romans had the concept of zero, just not a specific symbol for it. The zero symbol become important in positional notation, to keep the symbols in the right place.

An 8-bit processor can operate with 8-bit data, which can represent the unsigned integers from 0 to 255 decimal. If we need to represent the algebraic sign, we need to give up on bit, to represent -128 to +127, 0 being considered a positive number. The normal method of representing negative numbers is the 2's complement scheme.

There are many ways to do represent negative numbers. The case we are familiar with from our use of the decimal system is the use of a special symbol "-". This gives us the sign-magnitude format.

We could do this in binary as well, and, in addition, there are the 1's complement and 2's complement schemes of representing negative numbers. To form the 1's complement of a binary number, change all bits to their logical complement. Problem is, in a finite (closed) number system, the 1's complement system gives two different representations of zero (i.e., +0 and -0), both valid. To form the 2's complement, do the 1's complement and add 1. This is a more complex operation, but the advantage is, there is only one representation of zero. Because zero is considered a positive number, there is one more negative number than (non-zero) positive number in this representation. Two's complement has become the dominant choice for negative number representation in computers. An exercise for the student is to do subtraction by the addition of the 10's complement.

Integer Operations

The operations we want to do on integers include addition, subtraction, multiplication, and division. These are accomplished by the arithmetic-logic unit, the ALU. The ALU also implements logical operations on data, such as AND, OR, and Complement. Generally, the other processors that will be discussed do not include logical operations. The four basic math functions for integers can be implemented in terms of logic functions.

Floating point data format

This section describes the floating point number representation, and explains when it is used, and why. Floating point is an old computer technique for gaining dynamic range in scientific and engineering calculations, at the cost of accuracy. First, we look at fixed point, or integer, calculations to see where the limitations are. Then, we'll examine how floating point helps expand the limits. Most Graphic Processing Units do floating point.

In a finite word length machine, there is a trade-off between dynamic range and accuracy in representation. The value of the most significant bit sets the dynamic range because the effective value of the most positive number is infinity. The value of the least significant bit sets the accuracy, because a value less than the LSB is zero. And, the MSB and the LSB are related by the word length.

In any fixed point machine, the number system is of a

finite size. For example, in an 18-bit word, we can represent the positive integers from 0 to 2^{18}-1, or 262,143. A word of all zeros = 0, and a word of all ones = 262,143. I'm using 18 bits as an example because it's not too common. There's nothing magic about 8, 16, or 32 bit word sizes.

If we want to use signed numbers, we must give up one bit to represent the sign. Of course, giving up one bit halves the number of values available in the representation. For a signed integer in an 18-bit word, we can represent integers from + to - 131,072. Of course, zero is a valid number. Either the positive range or the negative range must give up a digit so we can represent zero. For now, let's say that in 18 bits, we can represent the integers from -131,072 to 131,071.

There are several ways of using the sign bit for representation. We can have a sign-magnitude format, a 1's complement, or a two's complement representation. Most computers use the 2's complement representation. This is easy to implement in hardware. In this format, to form the negative of a number, complement all of the bits (1->0, 0->1), and add 1 to the least significant bit position. This is equivalent to forming the 1's complement, and then adding one. One's complement format has the problem that there are two representations of zero, all bits 0 and all bits 1. The hardware has to know that these are equivalent. This added complexity has led to 1's complement schemes falling out of use in favor of 2's complement. In two's complement, there is one representation of zero (all bits zero), and one less positive number, than the negatives. (Actually, since zero is considered positive, there are the same number. But, the negative numbers have more range.) This is easily illustrated for 3-bit numbers, and can be extrapolated to any other fixed length representation.

Remember that the difference between a signed and an unsigned number lies in our interpretation of the bit pattern.

Up to this point we have considered the bit patterns to represent integer values, but we can also insert an arbitrary binary point (analogous to the decimal point) in the word. For integer representations, we have assumed the binary point to lie at the right side of the word, below the LSB. This gives the LSB a weight of 2^0, or 1, and the msb has a weight of 2^{16}. (The sign bit is in the 2^{17} position). Similarly, we can use a fractional representation where the binary point is assumed to lie between the sign bit and the MSB, the MSB has a weight of 2^{-1}, and the LSB has a weight of 2^{-17}.

The MSB sets the range, the LSB sets the accuracy, and the LSB and MSB are related by the word length. For cases between these extremes, the binary point can lie anywhere in the word, or for that matter, outside the word. For example, if the binary point is assumed to lie 2 bits to the right of the LSB, the LSB weight, and thus the precision, is 2^2. The MSB is then 2^{19}. We have gained dynamic range at the cost of precision. If we assume the binary point is to the left of the MSB, we must be careful to ignore the sign, which does not have an associated digit weight. For an assumed binary point 2 bit positions to the right of the MSB, we have a MSB weight of 2^{-3}, and an LSB weight of 2^{-20}. We have gained precision at the cost of dynamic range.

It is important to remember that the computer does not care where we assume the binary point to be. It simply treats the numbers as integers during calculations. We overlay the bit weights and the meanings.

Floating point operations

To add or subtract scaled values, they must have the same scaling factor; they must be commensurate. If the larger number is normalized, the smaller number must be shifted to align it for the operation. This may have the net result of adding or subtracting zero, as bits fall off the right side of the small word. This is like saying that 10 billion + .00001 is approximately 10 billion, to 13 decimal places of accuracy.

In multiplication, the scaling factor of the result is the sum of the scaling factors of the products. This is analogous to engineering notation, where we learn to add the powers of 10.

In division, the scaling factor of the result is the difference between the scaling factor of the dividend and the scaling factor of the divisor. The scaling factor of the remainder is that of the dividend. In engineering notation, we subtract the powers of 10 for a division.

In a normal form for a signed integer, the most significant bit is one. This says, in essence, that all leading zeros have been squeezed out of the number. The sign bit does not take part in this procedure. However, note that if we know that the most significant bit is always a one, there is no reason to store it. This gives us a free bit in a sense; the most significant bit is a 1 by definition, and the msb-1-th bit is adjacent to the sign bit. This simple trick has doubled the effective accuracy of the word, because each bit position is a factor of two.

The primary operation that will cause a loss of precision or accuracy is the subtraction of two numbers that have nearly but not quite identical values. This is commonly encountered in digital filters, for example, where successive readings are differenced. For an 18-bit word, if the readings differ in, say, the 19th bit position, then the difference will be seen to be zero. On the other hand, the scaling factor of the parameters must allow sufficient range to hold the largest number expected. Care must be taken in subtracting values known to be nearly identical. Precision can be retained by per-normalization of the arguments.

During an arithmetic operation, if the result is a value larger than the greatest positive value for a particular format, or less than the most negative, then the operation has overflowed the format. Normally, the absolute value function cannot overflow, with the exception of the absolute value of the least negative number, which has no corresponding positive representation.

In addition, the scaling factor can increase by one, if we consider the possibility of adding two of the largest possible numbers. We can also consider subtracting the largest (absolute value) negative number from the largest (in an absolute sense) negative number.

A one bit position left shift is equivalent to multiplying

by two. Thus, after a one position shift, the scaling factor must be adjusted to reflect the new position of the binary point. Similarly, a one bit position right shift is equivalent to division by two, and the scaling factor must be similarly adjusted after the operation.

Numeric overflow occurs when a nonzero result of an arithmetic operation is too small in absolute value to be represented. The result is usually reported as zero. The subtraction case discussed above is one example. Taking the reciprocal of the largest positive number is another.

As in the decimal representation, some numbers cannot be represented exactly in binary, regardless of the precision. Non-terminating fractions such as 1/3 are one case, and the irrational numbers such as e and pi are another. Operations involving these will result in inexact results, regardless of the format. However, this is not necessarily an error. The irrationals, by definition, cannot exactly be represented by a ratio of integers. Even in base 10 notation, e and pi extend indefinitely.

When the results of a calculation do not fix within the format, we must throw something away. We normally delete bits from the right (or low side) side of the word (the precision end). There are several ways to do this. If we simply ignore the bits that won't fit within the format, we are truncating, or rounding toward zero. We can choose the closest word within the format to represent the results. We can also round up by adding 1 to the LSB of the resultant word if the first bit we're going to throw away is a 1. We can also choose to round to even, round to odd, round to nearest, round towards zero, round towards + infinity, or round towards - infinity.

Consistency is the desired feature.

If we look at typical physical constants, we can get some idea of the dynamic range that we'll require for typical applications. The mass of an electron, you recall, is 9.1085 x 10-^{31} grams. Avogadro's number is 6.023 x 10^{23}. If we want to multiply these quantities, we need a dynamic range of 10$^{(23+31)}$ = 10^{54}, which would require a 180 bit word (10^{54} approx.= 2^{180}). Most of the bits in this 180 bit word would be zeros as place holders. Well, since zeros don't mean anything, can't we get rid of them? Of course.

We need dynamic range, and we need precision, but we usually don't need them simultaneously. The floating point data structure will give us dynamic range, at the cost of being unable to exactly represent data.

So, finally, we talk about floating point. In essence, we need a format for the computer to work with that is analogous to engineering notation, a mantissa and a power of ten. The two parts of the word, with their associated signs, will take part in calculation exactly like the scaled integers discussed previously. The exponent is the scaling factor that we used. Whereas in scaled integers, we had a fixed scaling factor, in floating point, we allow the scaling factor to be carried along with the word, and to change as the calculations proceed.

The representation of a number in floating point, like the representation in scientific notation, is not unique. For example,

6.54 x 10^2 = .654 x 10^3 = 654. x 10^0

We have to choose a scheme and be consistent. What is

normally done is that the exponent is defined to be a number such that the leftmost digit is non-zero. This is defined as the normal form.

In the floating point representation, the number of bits assigned to the exponent determines dynamic range, and the number of bits assigned to the mantissa determine the precision, or resolution. For a fixed word size, we must allocate the available bits between the precision (mantissa), and the range (exponent).

Granularity is defined as the difference between representable numbers. This term is normally equal to the absolute precision, and relates to the least significant bit.

The floating point unit can also implement *transcendental functions*. These are usually represented as Taylor series expansions of common trigonometric and log functions. Enough transcendentals are included to provide basis functions for all we might need to calculate.

- F2XM1 = 2^{X-1}
- FYL2X = Y * $\log_2$ (X)
- FYL2XP1 = Y * $\log_2$ (X+1)
- FPTAN = tangent
- FPATAN = arctangent

From the basis functions, if x=tan(a), then a = atan (x), and

- Sin (a) = x / sqrt (1 + x^2)
- Cos (a) = 1 / sqrt (1 + x^2)

15

$$\cdot \quad \text{Asin} (x) = \text{atan} [x / \text{sqrt} (1-x^2)]$$

There are known functions to calculate 2^x, e^x, 10^x, and y^x in terms of the F2MX1 (2^x-1) function. Similarly, the log base e and base 10 can be calculated in terms of the FYL2X (log base 2) function. All of the trigonometric, inverse trigonometric, hyperbolic, and inverse hyperbolic functions can be calculated in terms of the supplied basis functions.

Sometimes, it doesn't go quite right.

The floating point divide error in the Intel P5 Pentium processor evaded Intel's testing and user notice, until a Professor of Mathematics at Lynchburg College in Virginia, Thomas R. Nicely, noticed some inconsistencies in his calculations in October of 1994. He documented the cases and notified Intel. How many billions of financial and scientific/engineering calculations had been done with this chip previously, and the results accepted as good?

Intel had actually been aware of the problem since May, based on testing of the next generation chip, the Pentium Pro. Intel decided not to change the chip design, as the error was seen as minor, and the changing of the chip was an expensive and time consuming process. The problem gained widespread attention after a CNN report, and many computer users went back to double-check their calculations.

There was a large public outcry, and Intel agreed to replace the flawed chips upon request. This had a significant impact on Intel's bottom line, the company claiming $475 million. The problem was attributed to a error in a look-up table on the chip.

The problem can be demonstrated on Pentium's of clock speed 66 MHz or less, by doing the calculation 4195835 / 3145727. The correct answer is 1.3338204449136241002, but the chip will tell you its 1.33739068902037589. That's close enough, right? My H-P calculator says 1.33382045. My slide rule says 1.33.

So, what was designed or decided based on errors in the calculations? What financial calculations were effected? Small error multiplied by a billion equals...

Reference: Wolfe, Alexander, "Intel fixes a Pentium FPU glitch," Electronic Engineering Times, Nov. 7, 1994.

Denormalized numbers

This topic is getting into the number theory, and I will only touch on these special topics here. There is a use for numbers that are not in normal form, so-called de-normals. This has to do with decreasing granularity, and the fact that numbers in the range between zero and the smallest normal number. A denorm has an exponent which is the smallest representable exponent, with a leading digit of the mantissa not equal to zero. An un-normalized number, on the other hand, has the same mantissa case, but an exponent which is not the smallest representable. Let's get back to engineering.

If the result of an operation results in a number too large (in an absolute magnitude case) to be represented, we have generated an overflow. If the result is too small to be represented, we have an underflow. Results of an overflow can be reported as infinity (+ or - as required), or as an error bit pattern. The underflow case is where we have generated a denormalized number. The IEEE standard, discussed below, handles denorms as valid operands. Another approach is to specify resultant denorms as zero.

Infinities, overflows, and underflows.

Infinity is the largest number that can be represented in the number system. Adding 1 to infinity results in infinity, by definition. In a closed number system imposed by the finite word size of the computer, adding one to infinity results in an overflow, a change of sign.

Negative infinity is the most negative number that can be represented in the number system, not the smallest number.

The least positive number, or the smallest amount that can be represented in the finite number systems is 1. That is because the numbers are usually considered integers, with the binary point on the right of the word. In floating point representation it is different.

Overflow is the condition in a finite word size machine, where the result of an arithmetic operation is too large to fit in the word. For example, when adding two of the largest positive numbers in a 16-bit representation, the result would not fit in 16 bits. With the use of a two's complement representation scheme for negative numbers, the overflow would result in a sign change, from a large positive to a small negative number.

Overflows can be a problem, as the one that caused the premature termination of the Ariane 5 launch vehicle flight 501. The lost payload was worth more than $300 million.

Underflow is a condition where, as the result of an arithmetic operation, the result is smaller in value than the smallest representable number. The result will be reported as zero in integer representation, even if it is positive, greater than zero, but less than 1. The resolution of binary integers is 1.

Development of the IEEE standard

Standards help to keep everything consistent. We don't expect different answers from different brands of calculators. But back in the mainframe and minicomputer era, we got different answers based on the handling of floating point numbers differently by the various manufacturers. This is because a floating point value is not necessarily exact. It can be an approximation to the actual value. And, as calculations proceed, these same errors can add up. It was the same situation with the original implementations of floating point hardware chips. Different manufacturers handled situations such as rounding differently. Different answers resulted. That was to change in 1985, when the IEEE Standard for floating point was approved and adopted by industry.

Before that, portability of programs between different brands of computers had to be carefully checked, and, in some cases, re-coded.

In 1976, Intel was designing the floating point coprocessor for their x86 architecture. They were a key player in the early days of floating point, and their design would go on to heavily influence the standard. The standards effort spanned a decade, and had over 90 people involved directly.

One of the big issues that the standards committee tackled was the handling of underflow. This is the situation when a number gets close to zero, but is not actually zero. The number is not zero, but becomes smaller than the smallest representable number in the format. The standard does not guarantee a correct result. It does provide a level playing field of consistency and regularity.

The IEEE standard is revisited and modified as necessary about every ten to fifteen years. In 2008, a quad precision mode was added. Changes to the standard are handled very carefully, so as not to obsolete the millions upon millions of existing hardware units in use.

Signals data

In the computer, we generally deal with audio and video data, although we may be processing other signals as well. The signals data, if originally in analog form, would be converted to digital. Depending on the dynamic range required, the resultant data can be stored as integers, or floating point. This is the basis for Software Defined Radio (SDR).

Digital Signal Processing

Digital signal processors resemble computers in many ways, and come in embedded versions. They handle specialized data types, and include special-purpose operations derived from the digital signal processing realm. This includes the Multiply-and-Add (mac), a digital filtering primitive. DSP techniques for audio evolved from sonar processing, and video data processing evolved from radar.

A Digital Signal Processor (DSP) is similar to a general purpose CPU, but provides specialized operations for DSP-type operations on specialized data formats. Originally, the DSP function would be implemented by software running in a CPU. DSP operations usually have time deadline constraints (hard real time requirements).

Mobile phones and cable modems, to name two examples, drove the development of faster, dedicated hardware units. The first practical commercial product based on a DSP chip was Texas Instrument's Speak-n-Spell toy. Before that, the military applications of sonar and radar data processing drove the technology. Multicore chips for DSP are now common.

The nature of digital domain signal data and filtering in the digital domain require some unique architectural features. Hardware modulo addressing and bit-reversed addressing is used in digital filtering. Operations on data tend to be Single Instruction, Multiple Data (SIMD), which is explained below. The *Multiply-Accumulate* primitive is the basis for digital filter implementation. Saturation arithmetic is used to prevent overflow. Both fixed point and floating point data are used. A three-memory Harvard architecture allows simultaneous access of an opcode and two operands. DSP's can implement Forward and Inverse Discrete Sine and Cosine operations.

An illustrative device is Analog Devices' Blackfin series of embedded DSP's. These chips are supported by real-time operating systems. The Blackfin is a 32-bit RISC processor with dual 16-bit multiply-accumulate units, and provision for 8-bit video processing in real-time.

Some ARM chips such as the Cortex-8 family, and the OMAP3 processors include both a general purpose CPU, and a DSP.

Graphics Data Structure

Graphics data can be integer or floating point. Generally, it is organized in 1 dimensional arrays (vectors) or multi-dimensional arrays. Since we will see later that we can under use our GPU to do general purpose processing, there is nothing special about the data format. Keep in mind, the GPU does not implement logic functions.

To use the GPU in this way, we basically have to reformulate our computational problem in terms of the graphics operations the GPU provides. The OpenCL language, widely used in GPU programming, is general purpose.

Graphic Operations

Besides the usual add, subtract, multiply, and divide, there are some unique operations for graphics data. This include min, max, average, among others. We could accomplish these with a quick couple of lines of code, but it is much faster, once we develop the opcode to do it. Also, in graphics processing, it is common to have multiple units working on multiple data with the same operation at the same time.

Actually, before we discuss operations in the GPU, let's take a look at SIMD, one technique in parallel computing.

If one computer is fast, a bunch of them is faster, right? Yes, if we do it correctly. Massively parallel computers started out as large numbers of commodity computer boards, linked with a high speed interconnect. This evolved into commodity off-the-shelf microprocessors, using the same interconnects. The same technique is applicable to commodity GPU products. GPU's, as we cautioned, are not general purpose processors. However, they can address a large range of computationally intensive tasks if you format the data they way they expect it. They can cooperate with each other, if the necessary communication infrastructure is available. All this relies on the available of good software tools, and development environments.

The bottleneck to getting more than one processor to work on a given problem domain at one time is the communications. There is an upper bound in a bus-oriented, shared memory SMP systems, arising from the communication limit of the bus interconnect (a classic Shannon channel limit). Clusters of computers also suffer from an inter-processor communication limit, from the LAN-like interconnect. We can use a message passing approach, or shared memory for inter-processor communication. And keep in mind, each node of the architecture can be more than a single processor – we can have a mesh of meshes in a hierarchical fashion.

Another technique is to put multiple cpu/gpu units on a single chip, and use that as a node in a compute network. This is called Multicore technology. Multicore computer architecture uses two or more (up to 100's) of cpu's, configured into a multiprocessor on a single chip. Each cpu can fetch and execute its own instructions, and has a method to communicate with the other cpu's. If an embedded chip has a cpu, memory, and I/O on a single chip, a multicore architecture has an entire network of parallel processors on a single chip. In the same sense that a computer used to fill a room, then was reduced to a box, then to a chip, we now see a further reduction of multiple cpu's. It's just Moore's law. Every 18 months or so, the technology can give us a 2x factor of improvement. So far, so good.

For the longest time, the state of the technology only

allowed putting one cpu on a chip. As things progressed along the lines of Moore's Law, the separate floating point unit was incorporated onto the same chip. Then came cache memory. We are now at the point where we can put multiple cpu's on a chip; these being called cores. But just being able to cram more cpu's on a single piece of silicon doesn't solve our high-performance problem. There are bottlenecks introduced in this approach, and they must be addressed. This lesson was learned many years ago with multiprocessors. The technology has changed, but the architectural limitations are the same.

The limitations to computer performance tend to be either the instruction rate of the cpu itself, or the channel capacity of the various data paths involved. One approach to increased performance is parallelism.

Some performance enhancements come from the architecture of the multiprocessor. For example, interrupt processing can be offloaded to a non-busy cpu.

One issue is how interrupts are handled in multiprocessing. How are interrupts steered to the proper processor? It is a function of the operating system. In the same way that processes are assigned to certain processors, interrupts and their associated interrupt handling are also assigned. Binding interrupts to specific cpu's is not necessarily the proper approach; since this approach does not improve hits in cache memory Multiple interrupts can overload the selected processor. Handling interrupts is a task, and task allocation is a function of the operating system. A multiprocessing operating system is required to manage the unique issues of multiprocessor hardware.

Another issue is cache coherency. In multicore architectures, each CPU core has its own L1 cache, but shares L2 caches with other cores. Local data in the L1 caches must be consistent with data in other L1 caches. If one core changes a value in cache due to a write operation, that data needs to be changed in other caches as well (if they hold the same item).

This problem is well understood, and addressed by studies from the field of multiprocessing. The issues can be addressed by several mechanisms. In cache snooping, each cache monitors the others for changes. If a change in value is seen, the local cached copy is invalidated. This means it will have to be re-accessed from the next level before use. A global directory of cached data can also be maintained. Several protocols for cache coherency include MSI, MESI, and others.

A multicore processor has multiple cpu and memory elements in a single chip. Being on a single chip reduces the communications times between elements, and allows for multiprocessing. Advances in microelectronics fabrication techniques lead to the implementation of multicores for desktop and server machines around 2007. It was becoming increasingly difficult to increase clock speeds, so the obvious approach was to turn to parallelism. Currently, in this market, quad-core, 6-core, and 8-core chips are available. Besides additional cpu's, additional on-chip memory must be added, usually in the form of memory caches, to keep the processors fed with instructions and data. There is no inherent difference in multicore architectures and multiprocessing with single core chips, except in the speed of communications. The standard interconnect technologies used in multiprocessing and clustering are applied to inter-core communications.

We can compare multicore devices to large parallel machines of some 10 years past, in the same sense that we can compare a single-chip cpu to large mainframe systems of 20-25 years ago. Things have gotten smaller and more capable at the same time. What used to fill a room went to a file cabinet size, then a desktop box size, then to a single chip.

Coupling between cores can be tight or loose. A tightly coupled system usually is implemented with shared memory. A loosely coupled system generally uses communication channels between cores.

Actually, before we discuss operations in the GPU, let's take a look at SIMD, one technique in parallel computing.

SIMD

Intel x86 processors added a single-instruction multiple-data (SIMD) extension to the base architecture called MMX, MultiMedia Extension, in 1997. It included eight new 64-bit registers. These registers are meant to hold eight 8-bit integers, four 16-bit integers, or two 32-bit integers, which will be operated upon in parallel. After Intel received a license to build Arm processors, it added it's MMX architecture to the ARM world.

The MMX registers are actually mapped into the floating point registers, making it tricky to do floating point and MMX operations simultaneously. The floating point registers are 80 bits wide, and the MMX registers use the lower 64 bits. The MMX extension has continued in the IA-64, but a more SIMD operation for graphics are now included on most graphics cards.

MMX supports saturation arithmetic. In this scheme, all operations are limited to a fixed range between a defined minimum and maximum. Values beyond those limits are not recognized. The mathematical properties of associativity and distributivity are not applicable in saturation arithmetic. An alternative to saturation arithmetic is where the values wrap-around, which unfortunately changes the sign in twos-complement representation. For audio processing (louder-than-loud) and video processing (blacker-than-black), saturation arithmetic works fine. It's the issue of getting an answer "close enough" in the time allowed. Saturation arithmetic plays an important role in digital signal processing techniques for video and audio processing.

In 1997, AMD released an enhanced MMX architecture called 3DNow! which added 32-bit floating point to the MMX's integer operations.

In 1999, Intel went to the Streaming SIMD Extensions

(SSE) architecture with the Pentium-III, and later the SSE2 with the Pentium 4. This has new 128-bit registers, and a corresponding instruction set extension. An SSE and a floating point instruction cannot be issued in the same cycle, due to resource conflicts. SSE2 brought double precision floating point support. SSE has 70 additional instructions to support operations from digital signal processing and graphics. SSE3 added new digital signal processing features, and SSE4 added an instruction for vector dot product.

Advanced Vector Extensions (AVX) introduced a 256-bit data path, and 3-operand instructions. These are extensions to the x86 architecture. These units can operate on 256 or 512 bit data structures. AVX-2 extends integers to 256 bits, and adds bit manipulation and multiply. AVX-512 extends data and operations to 512 bits. Vector data can be loaded from non-contiguous memory locations, referred to as gather, and stored to non-contiguous locations, called scatter. Exponential and reciprocal instructions accelerate transcendental functions. They also implement the fused multiply-add operation, which looks like: $X = \text{round}\,(a \times b + c)$.

Graphics Processing Unit (GPU) Operations

The first processor to include a graphics unit was the Texas Instruments' TMS-34010 in 1986. Before this, a GPU was a separate chip. Now, the functionality has been included along with the cpu (which may have multiple cores). GPU's can be included with the cpu, or be a standalone unit.

A GPU is a specialized computer architecture to manipulate image data at high rates. The GPU devices are highly parallel, and specifically designed to handle image data, and operations on that data. They do this much fastest than a programmed general purpose CPU. Most desktop machines have the GPU function on a video card or integrated with their CPU. Originally, GPU's were circuit card based. Now, they're chips, and increasingly, multicore chips. GPU operations are very memory intensive. The GPU design is customized to SIMD type operations.

The instruction set of the GPU is specific to graphics operations on block data. The requirements were driven by the demands of 2-D and 3-D video games on pc's, phones, tablets, and dedicated gaming units. As GPU units became faster and more capable, they began to consume more power (and thus generate more heat) than the associated CPU's. The GPU operations are typically memory intensive, so fast access to memory is critical.

A GPU is generally a dataflow architecture, as opposed to a control-flow, Von Neumann machine. The instructions executed depend on the inputs, to the extent that the order of execution is non-deterministic. On general purpose machines implementing graphics processing code, the behavior would be deterministic.

Although designed to process video data, some GPU's have been used as adjunct data processors and accelerators in other areas involving vectors and matrices, such as the inverse discrete cosine transform. Types of higher-level processing implemented by GPU's include texture mapping, polygon rendering, object rotation, and coordination system transformation. They also support object shading operations, data oversampling, and interpolation. GPU's find a major application area in video decoding. Building on this, GPU's enable advanced features in digital cameras such as facial recognition, or eye tracking. GPU's can be used to accelerate database operations such as gather and scatter, vertex operations. A vertex is where lines (or vectors) meet. GPU's are enabling the optical lane departure feature on cars, and will help to enable self-driving cars.

GPU's can tackle the embarrassingly parallel problems in engineering and physics, those that map to multiple parallel tasks that can be executed simultaneously. Examples of some of these applications include protein folding and ray tracing. Practical, affordable systems are being built with hundred's of thousands of interconnected GPU's.

You can do general purpose computing on a GPU, although it may not be the ideal platform. It requires you to recast your computation in a way the GPU understands, which is to say, in terms of graphics. So, we might have to represent the data as a 2D or 3D object, that we can apply the GPU's operations on. GPU's are special purpose devices that have instruction sets that are not general purpose, and are intended specifically for graphics data processing, and problems that lend themselves to stream or vector processing. GPU's are stream processors, in that they operate in parallel on multiple data. Given the right problem, that is mapable into the GPU's architecture, a huge performance gain of orders of magnitude can be achieved, over regular CPU's.

One figure of merit in GPU's is their arithmetic intensity, defined as the number of operations per memory access. You might think of this as a computation:communication ratio.

GPU's are used for coordinate system transformations, and for science data processing. The GPU can implement such operations as shading, codec, mapping, video decoding, and 3D image manipulation. A big driver for the development and enhancement of GPU's is video games, and digital cameras and tv's.

Extensive code libraries exist for GPU's, and different problem domains, from physics modeling, to video gaming and virtual reality. API's include OpenGL and Directx. OpenGL, the Open (source) graphics libraries operate across languages and platforms. It was introduced in 1992. It is an industry standard, and claims scalability from hand-held to supercomputer. It consists of a series of library functions, callable from most computer languages. DirectX, similarly, has a set of runtime libraries. It is a Microsoft product. There are other libraries of graphics functions available as well.

GPU's need high bandwidth connections to data. They are beginning to include fast, hardware managed, multi-level caches. The architectures differ from that of general purpose caches, since the GPU is mostly accessing vector data, from consecutive memory locations. GPU's have large register files on chip to reduce access time to frequently used data.

GPU Clusters

CPU compute clusters, with supercomputer credentials, were built with commodity ALU chips with an appropriate communications infrastructure. For example, the Cray T3D machine used DEC Alpha 64 bit micros. Cray used the DEC Alpha chip in it's circa 1996 T3E. NEC pulled together a machine from MIPS R4000 processors. A favorite architecture in that era was the Inmos Transputer, a monolithic CPU and FPU, with four communications channels included. They also had a switching fabric that scaled. The author participated in a University project involving a 64 node machine of this design.

GPU clusters are large numbers of off-the-shelf GPU nodes with their associated memory and I/O in a cluster arrangement with very high bandwidth interconnect, such as Gigabit Ethernet or PCIe. They are supported by an operating system, GPU driver software from the board manufacturer, and a Clustering API. OpenCL has a clustering software product, VirtualCL. GPU clusters are being used in all areas of High Performance Computing.

Taxonomy of Systems

Multiprocessing allows us to apply the resources of multiple cpu's and their associated memory's to a single problem. If one cpu is fast, aren't more faster? Maybe.

Multiprocessing can be implemented as the execution of multiple concurrent processes, under the control of an operating system. It is not time-sharing or multitasking. Multiprocessors have, by definition, more than one processor.

Flynn's Taxonomy recognizes four classes of computing machines. These are single instruction-single data (SISD), like a single cpu, single instruction-multiple data (SIMD); multiple instruction-single data, and multiple instruction-multiple data. Multiprocessors are MIMD. SIMD machines execute the same sequence of instructions or thread on different data sets, as might be the case in vector processing. MISD is not seen much, but can be used to implement redundant computing.

MIMD does have challenges in the areas of resource contention, and the possibility of deadlock. Threads may contend for resources in a complex way that is difficult to manage globally. The Operating system is supposed to handle this. Semaphores are used to manage contention, much like in real-time operating systems.

All processors are the same in a symmetric

multiprocessor. We can have different processor types, in which case it is referred to as asymmetric. In core terms, we can have an asymmetric configuration with a cpu and a DSP.

Tightly coupled systems are connected by a bus, and use shared memory. A multicore architecture is a chip level multiprocessor. Tightly coupled systems have better performance, and have greater energy efficiency. Networks connect loosely coupled multiprocessors. A Cluster computer is an example.

Shared-memory MPP's usually do not have a homogeneous communication environment, due to communication bandwidth restrictions. A two tier communications architecture is used, with shared memory intrabox, and a lan-type point-point link for interbox messaging. Since MPP machines have to scale to thousands of processors, a distributed memory scheme is usually chosen. Another approach is to cluster SMP's. Data sharing is the key, and the critical issue for large parallel relational database applications. The performance will be made (or broken) by the sophistication of the interconnection scheme. Speed and latency are of critical importance. Latency predominates for short messages.

Consider the case of having to send a large volume of data from New York to California. We look at two options: we rent a gigabit class line, and transfer the data serially at OC-48, or about 2.4 gigabits per second. The latency, from the time a bit enters the line at New York until it exits at California, is very short, and depends on the time it takes light to traverse 2000 miles of cable. This is an expensive option. We could also decide to charter a 747 freighter, and load it with DVD's. Here, the latency is about 5 hours, but the data all arrives together. One case emphasizes speed, the other case emphasizes low latency.

A processing metric for throughput is typically given in gips and gflops. This may actually represent best case, guaranteed not-to-exceed no-ops per second. I/O throughput is typically given in gbytes /second. Storage is characterized by bytes, or, perhaps, bytes per unit volume. Of equal concern is memory volatility.

For the processor:I/O balance metric , we can use gips per gigabyte per second, similar to Kung's Alpha parameter. H. T. Kung worked on the iWarp architecture at Carnegie Mellon University. This simplifies to operations/byte, representing operations on every byte of throughput data. In signal processing capabilities, a number of 3-10 is typical. In computation environments such as statistics, a number like 10-100 is typical. At the other end of the spectrum, in data intensive environments, a number like 0.1 to 0.001 is more typical. The achievable Alpha depends heavily on whether a distributed or a shared memory architecture is used.

Scalable systems, those made up of multiple computational & communication building blocks, have an architecture that is responsive to the problem domain. In such a homogeneous system, the correct amount of processing and I/O can be provided for the initial requirements, with the ability to expand later in a building block fashion to address evolved requirements as well as redundancy or fault tolerance. Developing software for scalable systems is a challenge, mostly in deciding how the software is spread across the computational nodes. This is a solvable problem, based both on good software tools and on programmer experience. Research into these topics as well as the ability of the system itself to adapt to processing load, is ongoing. Transputer networks, discussed in chapter seven, use modular building blocks with integral communication capabilities to build networks that can offer linear problem speedup. This is obvious with compute-intensive, minimal communication tasks such as the Mandelbrot set, which could ideally use one processor element per pixel to calculate the image. Each point in the Mandelbrot set is independent of its neighbors. If we run a particular instance of the Mandelbrot set on a single cpu, then multiple units, and graph the run times against the number of processor elements, we will see a near-linear speedup. In the general case this is true, until the problem becomes more communication bound than compute bound. As a "best case", the Mandelbrot is an ideal benchmark; completely computationally intensive.

Media Processing

Media Processing refers to operations on audio and video data structures. These are Digital Signal Processing operations. Image compression and decompression operations on streaming video in real time is an example.

NXP Semiconductors, N.V. of the Netherlands integrates ARM Cortex cores with their signal processing technology.

The ARM NEON is a general purpose 128-bit SIMD engine operating on multimedia data structures. It has a 128-bit architecture, and serves as an extension for the ARM Cortex-A. It has sixteen 128-bit registers.

The Advanced SIMD extension, marketed as NEON technology provides standardized acceleration for media and signal processing applications. It is applicable to the ARM Cortex-A series. NEON can execute MP3 audio decoding on CPUs running at 10 MHz and can run the GSM AMR (Adaptive Multi-Rate) speech codec at no more than 13 MHz. It features a comprehensive instruction set, separate register files and independent execution hardware. NEON supports 8-, 16-, 32- and 64-bit integer and single-precision (32-bit) floating-point data and operates in SIMD operations for handling audio and video processing as well as graphics and gaming processing. In NEON, the SIMD supports up to 16 operations at the same time. The NEON hardware shares the same floating-point registers as used in VFP. The 32, 64-bit registers can be used as 16, 128 bit registers. Registers are used as vector data, all of the same type. Data types can be 8-, 16-, 32-, or 64-bit single precision floating point, signed or unsigned. It supports industry standards for Codecs, such as MPEG-4, H-264, and others. It implements 2D, 3D, and other vector operations. It is tightly coupled to the main ARM cpu. The register file is 128 bits wide.

The NEON is programmed in the c language, a vectorizing compiler, the OpenMAX DL library. It is supported in Android and Ubuntu linux.

There are many other programming languages that address the parallelization of resources such as the cpu. These include languages that explicitly express the parallelism of the problem, as well as extensions to common programming languages with parallelism features built-in.

Java supports a multi-threaded architecture, which can be mapped to multiple execution engines. Parallel-c has extensions to the language to allow aspects of parallelism to be expressed. So does some variations of Fortran and Modula (-3). There is also a Concurrent Pascal. Application languages such as LabView support parallelism. LabView has a dataflow architecture that maps well to parallel hardware.

Parallel-C supports architectures with the SMP/NUMA architecture, as well as the distributed memory model, like clusters. It is built on ISO-C, but includes an explicitly parallel execution model with a shared address space. It provides synchronization primitives and memory consistency. There are features for memory management and communications. Previously, Parallel-C operated with a pre-processor to first examine and exploit the parallelism of the problem. Unified Parallel C comes from the High Performance Computing Laboratory of the George Washington University.

Another language option is Co-array Fortran, an extension of Fortran-95. Fortran is alive and well, a favorite of big computation users. Co-array Fortran operates as if were replicated, and each copy executes simultaneously, with its own set of data.

nVidia's CUDA provides a parallel environment for GPU's. To go along with the hardware, nVidia provided massively parallel CDA-c, OpenCL, and DirectCompute software tools. These support not only parallelization, but also debugging of parallel code. GPU-trageted code can be developed by the same process and with the same look-and-feel tools as CPU code. Nvidia's Nexus development environment supported Microsoft Visual Studio, and C++.

We must consider the software tools to develop parallel applications to be of equal or greater importance than the hardware. We would like to have canned libraries of vector and matrix operations. We also could use vectorizing preprocessing compilers.

ARM

The XScale (ARM v5) effort at Intel was started after the purchase of DEC's StrongARM division in 1998, and Intels' inheritance of the license.

Multimedia extensions (Intel) MMX features for Xscale were also implemented as 43 new SIMD instructions containing the full MMX instruction set and the integer instructions from Intel's x86 SSE instruction set. This represents Intel's major contribution to the ARM. MMX also included new instructions unique to XScale. MMX provided 16 additional 64-bit registers that are treated as an array of two 32-bit words, four 16-bit half-words or eight 8-bit bytes. The XScale core can perform up to eight adds or four MACs in parallel in a single cycle. This capability was used to enhance speed in decoding and encoding of multimedia data and in game support. An internal 256 kB SRAM was included to reduce power consumption and latency due to off-chip memory.

NEON implements an advanced SIMD instruction set and was first introduced with the ARM Cortex −A8 model. This is an extension of the FPU with a quad Multiply-and-Accumulate (MAC) unit and additional 64-bit and 128-bit registers.

Single instruction, multiple data (SIMD) describes computers with multiple processing elements that perform the same operation on multiple data simultaneously. Thus, such machines exploit data level parallelism. Vector processing is where a single operation is applied to an entire 1-dimensional array of data.

The Cortex-A15 is multi-core, and has an out-of-order superscalar pipeline. The chip was introduced in 2012, and is available from TI, NVidia, Samsung, and others. It can address a terabyte of memory. The integer pipeline is 15 stages long, and the floating point pipeline is up to 25 stages. The instruction issue is speculative. There can be 4 cores per cluster, two clusters per chip. Each core has separate 32k data and instruction caches. The level-2 cache controller supports up to 4 megabytes per cluster. DSP and NEON SIMD are supported, as is floating point. Hardware virtualization support is included.

NEON source code can be ported to SIMD, by an Intel-supplied tool. Due to the differences in implementation, this is not a simple 1:1 translation. This involves redefining NEON-64 and -128 bit vectors in terms of x86 SIMD data format. Then, the function translation is done. Even with functions that correspond, there can be implementation-based behavioral differences. For example, when specification indices are out of bounds, NEON returns zero, but Intel sets the MSB. Actually, 128-bit performance increases, but 64-bit performance gain is less. Use of constants is problematic, because loading constants in a loop adds to the memory look-up overhead. It is better to synthesize constants in a loop.

(This reminds the author, and I'm dating myself, of running Fortran programs on both IBM and Univac Mainframes. Because the IBM was a 32-bit 2's complement machine, and the Univac was a 36 bit, 1's complement machine, the same source code would run, but you would get different results).

Vector Processor

Vector processing involves the processing of vectors of related data, in a SIMD (single-instruction, multiple-data) mode. For example, vector addition is an SIMD operation.

SIMD refers to a class of parallel computers that perform the same operations on multiple data items simultaneously. This is data level parallelism, which is found in multimedia (video and audio) data used in gaming applications. The SIMD approach evolved from the vector supercomputers of the 1970's, which operated upon a vector of data with a single operation. Sun Microsystems introduced SIMD operations in their SPARC architecture in 1995.

Examples

This section will discuss several approaches to implementation of GPU's.

The Raspberry Pi

The Raspberry Pi is a small, inexpensive, single board computer based on the ARM architecture. It is targeted to the academic market. It uses the Broadcom BCM2835 system-on-a-chip, which has a 700 MHz ARM processor, a video GPU, and currently 512 M of RAM. It uses an SD card for storage. The Raspberry Pi runs the

GNU/linux and FreeBSD operating systems. It was first sold in February 2012. Sales reached ½ million units by the Fall. Due to the open source nature of the software, Raspberry Pi applications and drivers can be downloaded from various sites. It requires a single power supply, and dissipates less than 5 watts. It has USB ports, and an Ethernet controller. It does not have a real-time clock, but one can easily be added. It outputs video in HDMI resolution, and supports audio output. I/O includes 8 general purpose I/O lines, UART, I2C bus, and SPI bus.

The Raspberry Pi design belongs to the Raspberry Pi Foundation in the UK, which was formed to promote the study of Computer Science. The Raspberry Pi is seen as the successor to the original BBC Microcomputer by Acorn, which resulted in the ARM processor. The unit has enough resources to host an operating system such as linux.

The B+ version of the Pi has a Image System Pipeline (ISP) to directly handle data from a digital camera, and can be programmed with OpenGL. This is a GPU with 20 processing stages. It can handle a frame rate of 30 per second, with 1080 pixel resolution. It uses 16-way vector code, and the pipeline operates at 250 Mhz.

CUDA

Cuda (Compute Unified Device Architecture) is the dominant proprietary GPU product from Nvidia. To go along with the hardware, nVidia provided massively parallel CDA-c, OpenCL, and DirectCompute software tools. These support not only parallelization, but also debugging of parallel code. GPU-targeted code can be developed by the same process and with the same look-and-feel tools as CPU code. Nvidia's Nexus development environment supports Microsoft Visual Studio, and C++. MATLAB provides a Parallel Computing Toolbox. Nvidia pioneered the use of GPU accelerators in 2007. They come with a set of optimized libraries, and parallization tools.

CUDA is a trademark of nVidia Corporation. It is a parallel computing platform and a programming model. It enables dramatic increases in computing performance by harnessing the power of the graphics processing unit. A CUDA program includes parallel functions (kernels) across parallel threads. The compiler organizes these threads into blocks and grids. A block is a set of concurrently executing threads that can synchronize and co-ordinate. A grid is an array of blocks. In the CUDA programming model a thread has private memory. Each block has shared memory space, as do Grids.

Threads map to processors. Each Gpu unit executes one or more grids. Each streaming multiprocessor executes one or more thread blocks, and CUDA cores, and possibly other execution engines, execute threads.

CUDA introduced a variation on the digital signal processing Multiply-Accumulate operation (AxB+C), called Fused Multiply-ADD (FMA). In traditional Multiply-Add the AxB product will be truncated, but in the FMA, all bits of the produce are retained for the ADD operation.

The implementation of floating point on CUDA is not completely, but mostly IEEE compliant. This approach varies with vendor. Most GPU's at this time do not fully support 64-bit floating point data and operations.

Applying the horsepower of the GPU to real problems, the CUDA allows applications to be written in c, c++, Python, and FORTRAN. NVIDIA unveiled CUDA in 2006 as a solution for general-computing on GPU's.

The G-80 chip, introduced in 2006, established the GPU computing model. It supported the c programming language, and was threaded. It implemented the Single Instruction, Multiple Thread (SIMT) concept. It had a complexity of 680 million-1.4 billion transistors. It did not include L1 or L2 cache.

Fermi

The Fermi architecture was released in 2010, as a significant improvement over the G-80. It implemented up to 512 CUDA cores, each executing an integer or floating point operation per clock. It required 3 billion transistors. The chip supported c++, OpenCL, and DirectCompute. It featured full IEEE floating point, single and double precision. It implemented on-chip L1 and L2 caches. The GigaThread™ engine allowed for concurrent kernel execution, and out-of-order thread block execution. The architecture was 32-bit. A new instruction set architecture (ISA) supported parallel thread execution via a virtual machine.

Kepler

The Kepler GK110 CUDA chip is constructed from over 7 billion transistors, and provides a TeraFlop (10^{12}) of double-precision floating point operations per second. This is a performance increase of a factor of three over its predecessor, the Fermi model. The high-end model includes dynamic parallelism, which adjusts and controls the scheduling in the GPU without the intervention of the CPU. GPU utilization is enhanced by a technique known as Hyper-Q, which allows multiple cpu cores to use a single GPU, up to 32.

The unit can include up to 15 SMX processor units, and six 64-bit memory controllers. There is a 1536 kbytes of L2 Cache on chip. SMX is nVidia's term for the Streaming Microprocessor architecture. SMX has 8 instruction dispatch engines, a 32-bit register files of size 65,536, 64 kbytes of shared memory/L1 cache, and a 48k read-only data cache. This cache is reserved for data values known (by the compiler) not to change, and thus no cache writes are required. The unit also includes 192 CUDA cores, 64 double-precision arithmetic units, 32 special function units (SFU), and 32 load/store units. The CUDA cores include both integer and floating point capability. The special function units assist in transcendental computations.

A group of 32 threads than can operate in parallel is called a warp. Up to 4 warps can be executing simultaneously. Thread scheduling is done in hardware, but based on information from the compiler ("hints') concerning dependencies and data hazards. The compiler is a critical part of scheduling threads for best efficiency. A special instruction allows executing threads to share data without going through shared memory. Atomic memory operations are provided to ensure consistency among threads. Texture filtering units (TFU's) are provided in the architecture.

Radeon

Radeon is an other major manufacturer of high end GPU cards, starting in the year 2000. Radeon is now a division of AMD. They are supported by a proprietary software device driver package called Radeon Software, Crimson edition. This runs on Microsoft operating systems, or linux. There is also an open source tool, the Direct Rendering Infrastructure.

AMD's accelerated processing unit (APU) is a 64-bit CPU and graphics accelerator. It is based on the Heterogeneous System Architecture (HSA) standard. It allows for the CPU and GPU to operate on the same bus, with shared memory. ARM is also a member of the HSA Foundation. The graphics cpu also does the floating point operations. AMD calls it the STREAM technology, and it is supported with OpenCL.

Intel GPU's

Intel is currently in its 10th generation of GPU's. The first-gen unit, the Intel 740 dates to 1998, and was supported by OpenGL. By the fifth generation, in 2010, each execution engine had a 128 bit wide floating point unit, that executed four 32-bit operations per clock. By the eighth generation, each EU had dual SIMD-4 FPU's, with clock rates below a gigahertz.

Intel implements Imagination Technologies PowerVR architecture under license. This architecture supports very high speed 3D rendering. Now in their 8th generation, some of the family members are achieving 25 gflops, with an architecture for Apple capable of 360 Gflops.

GPU computing

The focus on large parallel machines has changed from clusters of general purpose ALU's to GPU's. This has taken over the field of high performance computing.

The graphics processing unit performs arithmetic operations on image data. These were introduced in the late 1990's as specialized architectures optimized for processing of large blocks of graphics data in parallel. Their instruction set is targeted to operations performed on 3D graphics data, such as transformations and rendering. Although these were originally targeted to computer gaming applications, it was not lost on scientists and engineers that this was the type of matrix manipulation and digital filtering that they employed in many different areas. The GPU is not general-purpose, but is targeted and optimized to operate on matrix data structures. GPU's are now used for many general-purpose scientific and engineering computing across a range of platforms. The term GPU was invented by high-performance graphics vendor nVidia.

Using high-level languages, GPU-accelerated applications can run the sequential part of the workload on a CPU, optimized for single-threaded performance, while running parallel processing on the GPU. This is called referred to as "GPU computing."

GPU computing is possible because today's GPU does a lot more than just render graphics: It might achieve a teraflop of floating point performance.

The first GPU's were designed as graphics accelerators, supporting only specific fixed-function pipelines. Starting in the late 1990s, the hardware became increasingly programmable. Less than a year after the GPU first appeared, it was being applied in various technical computing fields because of its excellent floating point performance. The General Purpose GPU, GPGPU as nVidia calls it, had appeared. Derived from that, we get GPU-accelerated computing.

Initially, GPU's ran graphics programming languages such as OpenGL. Developers had to map scientific calculations onto problems that could be represented by triangles and polygons. A breakthrough came when a group of Stanford University researchers set out to re-purpose the GPU as a "streaming processor." What's in a name?

In 2003, *Brook* was introduced as the first widely adopted programming model to extend C with data-parallel constructs. Using concepts such as streams, kernels, and reduction operators, the Brook compiler and runtime system presented the GPU as a general-purpose processor in a high-level language. Most importantly, Brook programs were not only easier to write than hand-tuned GPU code, they were many times faster. GPU's process high speed video data on phones, tablets, and tv's, and also find wide application in scientific and financial computing. GPU-based supercomputers are tackling the hard problems, such as SETI- the search for extra-terrestrial intelligence, protein folding, weather forecasting, financial modeling and analysis, and oil and gas exploration.

GPU-based Supercomputers

To give you an idea how mainstream this topic is, just go shopping for "gpu supercomputer" on Google. You'll be amazed how affordable they are. Nvidia has a page on building your own personal supercomputer, based on the Tesla.
(www.nvidia.com/object/tesla_build_your_own.html).
Motherboard manufacturer Asus offers a supercomputing workstation with 7 PCIe slots on the motherboard for the Tesla boards. The heat-pipe based cooling system, and the power supply are well matched to the compute architecture. The motherboard supports an Intel Xenon processor, and triple channel DDR-3 memory.

The Register (www.theregister.co.uk) reported in

September of 2015 on "Nine of the world's fastest GPU supercomputers." They mention that of the Top 500 list of supercomputers, 52 used the nVidia GPU.

Let's look at number one (in 2015), the Oak Ridge National Lab's *Titan,* a Cray XL7. It achieved over 17 Petaflops per second, using 262,632 NVIDIA K20x GPU's. It consumes a mere 8.2 Megawatts of power (well, there is a downside). Although, it is one of the most energy efficient machines in the area of Gigaflops per watt, coming in at 2.1. It will be replaced by a faster machine in 2018. A similar Cray XC30 at the Swiss National Supercomputing Centre uses 73,808 of the GPU's to achieve 6.2 Pflops. A commercial system in Australia is a used for stock trading. It is a SGU ICE-X/Superblade, with more than 265,000 cores, achieving 3.5 Petaflops.

Intel is a player in the Supercomputer world, with units based on its Xeon and Xenon-Phi X-86-64 architectures, with the AVX-512 extensions. The Phi current high end model, the 7250, has 68 cores, supported with 34 megabytes of L2 cache. Each operates at 1.4 GHz, with a turbo burst frequency of 1.6. These chips dissipate in excess of 200 watts. The Phi series does not currently support virtualization. They can support a total of 284 gigabytes of memory, on 6 channels. These cpu's are the backbone of Intel's Scalable System Framework (SSF).

Rad-Hard GPU's

The GPU architecture has been instantiated into radiation hardened versions, opening a new niche and market. GPU's are used on Earth to very quickly analyze images. Now that stage can be done in orbit, or at a far-away planet, and minimize transmit bandwidth and time.

Images can be processed in situ, and only the appropriate ones telemetered. Taking it a step further, Nvidia has a AI board for satellite applications. The Tegra TX2I can achieve 1.3 Teraflops. It is available as a System-on-a-module, The S-A1760 Venus. It is applicable for use in low earth orbit. Aitech has a space GPGPU, based on the Nvidia device.

Wrap-up

GPU's are specialized processors that find a home in processing media data, audio, and video. They are faster at that than a programmed general purpose CPU. They support data structures and instructions that are unique to the problem domain. They support integer and floating point, but they are best at vectors. There main mode of operation is Single Instruction, Multiple Data, where a single operation is applied across many data points. We will be seeing more of these units becoming mainstream, as the cost of the technology comes down, and they enable more applications on the consumer market. GPU's are currently dominant in supercomputing, but there has been a bit of a steep implementation curve, eased somewhat by manufacturer-supplied migration tools. Don't count out traditional compute architectures on steriods. Watch for ORNL's old machine to appear on E-bay.

References

Barlas, Gerassimos *Multicore and GPU Programming: An Integrated Approach,* Morgan Kaufmann, 1ˢᵗ ed, 2014, ISBN-978-0124171374.

Bruhn, Fredrik C.; Nandinbaatar Tsog; Kunkel, Fabian; Flordal, Oskar; Troxel, Oskar; *Enabling radiation tolerant heterogeneous GPU-based onboard data processing in space, CEAS Space J.***12**, 551–564 (2020). https://doi.org/10.1007/s12567-020-00321-9

Cai, Yiyu; See, Simon *GPU Computing and Applications*, Springer, 2015, ISBN-978-9811013607.

Cavanagh, Joseph J. F. *Digital Computer Arithmetic Design and Implementation*, 1984, McGraw Hill, ISBN 0-07-010282-1.

Cook, Shane *CUDA Programming: A Developer's Guide to Parallel Computing with GPUs,* 1ˢᵗ edition, Morgan Kaufmann, 2012, ISBN-978-0124159334.

Flores, Ivan T*he Logic of Computer Arithmetic*, 1963, Prentice-Hall, ISBN 0135400392.

Kindratenko, Volodymyr (Ed) *Numerical Computations with GPUs*, Springer, 2014, ISBN-978-3319065472.

Hwang, Kai *Computer Arithmetic, Principles, Architecture, and Design,* Wiley, 1979, ISBN

0471034967.

Jaraweh, Yaser, et al "Gpu-based Personal Supercomputing," 2013, IEEE, Applied Electrical Engineering and Computing Technologies (AEECT).

Kindratenko, Volodymyr V. et all, "GPU Clusters for High-Performance Computing,"
avail:
www.ncsa.illinois.edu/People/kindr/papers/ppac09_paper.pdf

Kirk, David B.; Hwu, Wen-mei, W. *Programming Massively Parallel Processors: A Hands-on Approach,* Morgan Kaufmann, 1ˢᵗ ed, 2010, ISBN-978-0123814722

Kurzak, Jakub; Bader, David A.; Dongarra, Jack (Eds) *Scientific Computing with Multicore and Accelerators* ,CRC Press; 1st edition (December 7, 2010), ISBN 143982536X.

Muller, Jean-Michel et al, *Handbook of Floating Point Arithmetic*, 2009, Birkhauser, ISBN 081764704X.

Newmarch, Jan *Raspberry Pi GPU Audio Video Programming,* 1st ed., 2016, Apress, ISBN-978-1484224717.

Overton, Michael L. *Numerical Computing with IEEE Floating Point Arithmetic*, Society for Industrial & Applied Math; 1st ed, April 2001, ISBN- 978-

0898714821.

Powell, Wesley; Campola, Michael; Sheets, Teresa; Davidson, Abigail Commercial, NASA/GSFC "Off the shelf GPU Qaulification for Space Applications," 2018, https://ntrs.nasa.gov/api/citations/20180006906/downloads/20180006906.pdf

Scott, Norman R. *Computer Number Systems & Arithmetic*, 1984, Prentice-Hall, ISBN-0-13-164211-1.

Sheppard, Andrew *Programming GPUs,* 2011, O'Reilly Media, ISBN 1449302351.

Soyata, Tolga *Introduction to CUDA and GPU Programming*, Chapman and Hall/CRC, May 2017, ISBN-978-1498750752.

Aiken, Ales; Banerjee, Utpal *Instruction Level Parallelism*, Springer, 1st ed, 2016, ISBN-978-1489977953.

Stakem, Patrick H. *Floating Point Computation,* PRRB Publishing, 2014, ISBN – 9781520216195.

Stakem, Patrick H. *Multicore Computer Architectures,* 2014, PRRB Publishing, ISBN-9781520241371.

Storti, Duane; Yurtoglu, Mete, *CUDA for Engineers: An Introduction to High-Performance Parallel Computing*, Addison Wesley Professional, 1st ed, 2015, 978-0134177410.

Suh, Jung W., Kim, Youngmin, *Accelerating MATLAB with GPU Computing: A Primer with Examples*, Morgan Kaufmann, 1st ed, 2013, ISBN-978-0124080805.

Tan, Ying *GPU-based Parallel Implementation of Swarm Intelligence Algorithms*, 2016, 1st ed, Morgan Kaufmann, ISBN-978-0128093627.

Wilt, Nicholas, The *CUDA Handbook: A Comprehensive Guide to GPU Programming,* 1st ed, Addison-Wesley Professional, ISBN-978-0321809469.

Yuen, David A. (ed) *GPU Solutions to Multi-scale Problems in Science and Engineering*, Springer, 2013, ISBN-978-3642164040.

Zhislina, Victoria, "From ARM NEON to Intel SSE – the automatic porting solution, tips and tricks," Intel, Dec. 12, 2012. avail: https://software.intel.com/

Wikipedia, various.

There are numerous books on OpenGL and DirectX programming. Check Amazon.com.

Glossary

1's complement – signed integer format that forms the negative by logically inverting all the bits. There are, unfortunately, 2 different values of zero.

2's complement – signed integer format in which a negative is formed by doing the 1's complement, and then adding 1. There is only 1 representation of zero.

2-d – two dimensional.

3-d – three dimensional.

ASIC - application specific integrated circuit

ALU – arithmetic-logic unit, does arithmetic and logical operations on data.

AMD – Advanced Micro Devices (Company).

API – applications program interface, a set of routines, protocols, and tools for building software applications.

APU – accelerated processing unit (AMD).

ARM – originally, Acorn Risc Machines.

Asin – arc sine.

AVX – advanced vector extensions (Intel).

BBC - British Broadcasting Corporation.

Big-endian - having the least significant byte in a word on the right.

Bit - the smallest unit of binary information.

BLOB - Binary Large Object, usually applied to image data.

Byte - a collection of 8 bits

Cache- a small, fast memory between the processor and the main memory.

Codec – coder/decoder. For example, for MPEG.

Control Flow – computer architecture involving directed flow through the program; data dependent paths are allowed.

Coprocessor – another processor to supplement the operations of the main processor. Used for floating point, video, etc. Usually relies on the main processor for instruction fetch and control.

CPU – central processing unit.

CUDA - Compute Unified Device Architecture, from Nvidia.

Dataflow – a computer architecture that allows concurrent execution; sometimes called stream processing.

Data parallelism – data distributed across nodes in a parallel architecture.

DCT – discrete cosine transformation.

Denorm – in floating point representation, a non-zero number with a magnitude less than the smallest normal number.

DMA - direct memory addressing - I/O to/from memory without processor involvement.

DSP – Digital Signal Processing.

EU – execution unit. Contains the ALU and registers, and maybe the FPU.

Exception – interrupt due to internal events, such as overflow, or attempted division by zero.

Fixed point – computer numeric format with a fixed number of   digits or bits, and a fixed radix point. Integers.

Floating Point - a scientific/engineering numeric representation scheme with a mantissa and an exponent.

FPU – floating point unit – does math operations on floating point formatted data.

Frame buffer – implemented in RAM, contains a bitmap and a complete frame of data.

Gather – loading vector data from non-contiguous memory locations.

GFLOPS - Giga (10^9) Floating Point Operations per second.

GIPS - Giga (10^9) Operations per second.

GPGPU – general purpose (computing) on graphics processing units.

GPU – graphics processing unit, ALU for graphics data. nVidia.

GPU cluster – compute nodes and fast interconnect, a classic MPMS.

GUI – Graphical User Interface.

Harvard architecture – memory storage scheme with separate Instructions and data.

HDMI – High Definition Multimedia Interface.

HPC – high performance computing.

HSA – Heterogeneous System Architecture.

I2C – Inter-Integrated Circuit interface. A short-range serial link, using a multi-master bus.

IDCT – inverse discrete cosine transformation.

IEEE- Institute of Electronic and Electronic Engineers.

Integer – the natural numbers, zero, and the negatives of the natural numbers.

Interrupt – an asynchronous event to signal a need for attention (example: the phone rings).

IP – intellectual property.

ISA – instruction set architecture.

ISP – Image System Pipeline (ARM).

JPEG - Joint Photographic Experts Group.

L1 – cache closest to the CPU.

L2 – cache next in line.

LEO - Low Earth orbit.

Little-endian - having the least significant byte of a word on the right.

Logical operation – AND, OR, Exclusive OR, Negate.

LSB – least significant bit or byte.

MAC – multiply-accumulate, a primitive operation in

signal processing.

Mainframe – a computer you can't lift.

Mantissa – significant digits (as opposed to the exponent) of a floating point value.

MC – motion compensation.

Microprocessor – a monolithic CPU on a chip.

MIPS – millions of instructions per second; sometimes used as a measure of throughput.

MISD – multiple instruction, single data

MMU - memory management unit, translates virtual to physical addresses.

MMX – (Intel) multimedia extensions (to the instruction set and data formats.

MPE – Media Processing Engine.

MPEG – motion picture experts group – standards for audio and video compression and transmission.

MPMS – massively parallel microprocessor system.

MPP – Massively parallel processor.

MSB – most significant bit or byte.

Multicore – multiple processing cores on one substrate or chip; need not be identical.

NaN not-a-number (bit pattern used for status in floating point).

NEO - near Earth orbit.

NEON – instruction set for SIMD processing (ARM).

Normalized number – in the proper format for floating point representation.

OMAP – Open Multimedia Applications Platform. (Texas Instruments)

Open source – methodology for hardware or software development with free distribution and access.

ORNL – Oak Ridge National Lab, U.S. National Laboratory of the Department of Energy.

Overflow - the result of an arithmetic operation exceeds the capacity of the destination.

PCIe – Peripheral Component Interconnect Express. A serial bus.

PE - processor element, usually consisting of cpu, memory, I/O.

Paradigm – a pattern or model

Paradigm shift – a change from one paradigm to another. disruptive or evolutionary.

Parallel – multiple operations or communication proceeding simultaneously.

Petaflops – 10^{15} floating point operations per second.

PPU - Physics processing unit; does rigid and non-rigid body dynamics, fluid dynamics, finite element analysis, etc. GPU-based.

Rasterization – process in which geometric shapes are converted to pixels, for display.

Register – temporary storage location for a data item.

Reset – signal and process that returns the hardware to a

known, defined state.

RISC – reduced instruction set computer.

Scatter – storing a vector data in non-contiguous memory locations.

SDR – software defined radio.

SFU – Special Function Unit.

Sign-Magnitude – data format which has a sign bit, and an integer value.

SIMD – Single Instruction, Multiple Data. An operation on Vector data types.

SIMT – single instruction, multiple thread.

SMP - symmetric multi processor, or processing.

SMX – Streaming Microprocessor architecture, nVidia.

SOC – system on chip.

SPI – Serial Peripheral Interface (bus): short distance, synchronous serial.

Sqrt – square root

SSE - Streaming SIMD Extensions (SSE) – Intel.

Stream - sequence of data, requiring identical or similar processing.

Stream processor – a dataflow machine; In a stream processor, a sequence of operations is performed on each item in the stream.

Texturing – computing the colors of rendered surfaces.

TFU – texture filtering unit.

UART – Universal Asynchronous Receiver-Transmitter.

Underflow – the result of an arithmetic operation is smaller than the smallest representable number.

Vector – a collection of similar data in a one dimensional array.

Vector processor – a unit that does operations on vectors of data.

Von Neumann computer architecture, control flow, data and instructions share memory

VPU – Vision processing unit (ATI Technologies); a GPU.

Wiki – the Hawaiian word for "quick." Refers to a collaborative content website.

Word – a collection of bits of any size; does not have to be a power of two.

Zero address – architecture using implicit addressing, like a stack.

If you enjoyed this book, you might also be interested in some of these.

16-bit Microprocessors, History and Architecture, 2013 PRRB Publishing, ISBN-1520210922.

4- and 8-bit Microprocessors, Architecture and History, 2013, PRRB Publishing, ISBN-152021572X,

Apollo's Computers, 2014, PRRB Publishing, ISBN-1520215800.

The Architecture and Applications of the ARM Microprocessors, 2013, PRRB Publishing, ISBN-1520215843.

Earth Rovers: for Exploration and Environmental Monitoring, 2014, PRRB Publishing, ISBN-152021586X.

Embedded Computer Systems, Volume 1, Introduction and Architecture, 2013, PRRB Publishing, ISBN-1520215959.

The History of Spacecraft Computers from the V-2 to the Space Station, 2013, PRRB Publishing, ISBN-1520216181.

Floating Point Computation, 2013, PRRB Publishing, ISBN-152021619X.

Architecture of Massively Parallel Microprocessor

Systems, 2011, PRRB Publishing, ISBN-1520250061.

Multicore Computer Architecture, 2014, PRRB Publishing, ISBN-1520241372.

Personal Robots, 2014, PRRB Publishing, ISBN-1520216254.

RISC Microprocessors, History and Overview, 2013, PRRB Publishing, ISBN-1520216289.

*Robots and Telerobots in Space Application*s, 2011, PRRB Publishing, ISBN-1520210361.

The Saturn Rocket and the Pegasus Missions, 1965, 2013, PRRB Publishing, ISBN-1520209916.

Visiting the NASA Centers, and Locations of Historic Rockets & Spacecraft, 2017, PRRB Publishing, ISBN-1549651205.

Microprocessors in Space, 2011, PRRB Publishing, ISBN-1520216343.

Computer *Virtualization and the Cloud*, 2013, PRRB Publishing, ISBN-152021636X.

What's the Worst That Could Happen? Bad Assumptions, Ignorance, Failures and Screw-ups in Engineering Projects, 2014, PRRB Publishing, ISBN-1520207166.

Computer Architecture & Programming of the Intel x86

Family, 2013, PRRB Publishing, ISBN-1520263724.

The Hardware and Software Architecture of the Transputer, 2011,PRRB Publishing, ISBN-152020681X.

Mainframes, Computing on Big Iron, 2015, PRRB Publishing, ISBN- 1520216459.

Spacecraft Control Centers, 2015, PRRB Publishing, ISBN-1520200617.

Embedded in Space, 2015, PRRB Publishing, ISBN-1520215916.

A Practitioner's Guide to RISC Microprocessor Architecture, Wiley-Interscience, 1996, ISBN-0471130184.

Cubesat Engineering, PRRB Publishing, 2017, ISBN-1520754019.

Cubesat Operations, PRRB Publishing, 2017, ISBN-152076717X.

Interplanetary Cubesats, PRRB Publishing, 2017, ISBN-1520766173 .

Cubesat Constellations, Clusters, and Swarms, Stakem, PRRB Publishing, 2017, ISBN-1520767544.

Graphics Processing Units, an overview, 2017, PRRB Publishing, ISBN-1520879695.

Intel Embedded and the Arduino-101, 2017, PRRB Publishing, ISBN-1520879296.

Orbital Debris, the problem and the mitigation, 2018, PRRB Publishing, ISBN-*1980466483.*

Manufacturing in Space, 2018, PRRB Publishing, ISBN-1977076041.

NASA's Ships and Planes, 2018, PRRB Publishing, ISBN-1977076823.

Space Tourism, 2018, PRRB Publishing, ISBN-1977073506.

STEM – Data Storage and Communications, 2018, PRRB Publishing, ISBN-1977073115.

In-Space Robotic Repair and Servicing, 2018, PRRB Publishing, ISBN-1980478236.

Introducing Weather in the pre-K to 12 Curricula, A Resource Guide for Educators, 2017, PRRB Publishing, ISBN-1980638241.

Introducing Astronomy in the pre-K to 12 Curricula, A Resource Guide for Educators, 2017, PRRB Publishing, ISBN-198104065X.
Also available in a Brazilian Portuguese edition, ISBN-1983106127.

Deep Space Gateways, the Moon and Beyond, 2017, PRRB Publishing, ISBN-1973465701.

Exploration of the Gas Giants, Space Missions to Jupiter, Saturn, Uranus, and Neptune, PRRB Publishing, 2018, ISBN-9781717814500.

Crewed Spacecraft, 2017, PRRB Publishing, ISBN-1549992406.

Rocketplanes to Space, 2017, PRRB Publishing, ISBN-1549992589.

Crewed Space Stations, 2017, PRRB Publishing, ISBN-1549992228.

Enviro-bots for STEM: Using Robotics in the pre-K to 12 Curricula, A Resource Guide for Educators, 2017, PRRB Publishing, ISBN-1549656619.

STEM-Sat, Using Cubesats in the pre-K to 12 Curricula, A Resource Guide for Educators, 2017, ISBN-1549656376.

Embedded GPU's, 2018, PRRB Publishing, ISBN-1980476497.

Mobile Cloud Robotics, 2018, PRRB Publishing, ISBN-1980488088.

Extreme Environment Embedded Systems, 2017, PRRB Publishing, ISBN-1520215967.

What's the Worst, Volume-2, 2018, ISBN-1981005579.

Spaceports, 2018, ISBN-1981022287.

Space Launch Vehicles, 2018, ISBN-1983071773.

Mars, 2018, ISBN-1983116902.

X-86, 40th Anniversary ed, 2018, ISBN-1983189405.

Lunar Orbital Platform-Gateway, 2018, PRRB Publishing, ISBN-1980498628.

Space Weather, 2018, ISBN-1723904023.

STEM-Engineering Process, 2017, ISBN-1983196517.

Space Telescopes, 2018, PRRB Publishing, ISBN-1728728568.

Exoplanets, 2018, PRRB Publishing, ISBN-9781731385055.

Planetary Defense, 2018, PRRB Publishing, ISBN-9781731001207.

Exploration of the Asteroid Belt, 2018, PRRB Publishing, ISBN-1731049846.

Terraforming, 2018, PRRB Publishing, ISBN-1790308100.

Martian Railroad, 2019, PRRB Publishing, ISBN-1794488243.

Exoplanets, 2019, PRRB Publishing, ISBN-1731385056.

Exploiting the Moon, 2019, PRRB Publishing, ISBN-1091057850.

RISC-V, an Open Source Solution for Space Flight Computers, 2019, PRRB Publishing, ISBN-1796434388.

Arm in Space, 2019, PRRB Publishing, ISBN-9781099789137.

Search for *Extraterrestrial Life*, 2019, PRRB Publishing, ISBN-978-1072072188.

Submarine Launched Ballistic Missiles, 2019, ISBN-978-1088954904.

Space Command, Military in Space, 2019, PRRB Publishing, ISBN-978-1693005398.

Robotic Exploration of the Icy moons of the Gas Giants, ISBN- 979-8621431006.

History & Future of Cubesats, ISBN-978-1986536356.

Robotic Exploration of the Icy Moons of the Ice Giants, by Swarms of Cubesats, ISBN-979-8621431006.

Swarm Robotics, ISBN-979-8534505948.

Introduction to Electric Power Systems, ISBN-979-8519208727.

Powerships, Powerbarges, Floating Wind Farms: electricity when and where you need it, 2021, PRRB Publishing, ISBN-979-8716199477.

Centros de Control: Operaciones en Satélites del Estándar CubeSat (Spanish Edition), 2021, ISBN-979-8510113068.

The Artemis Missions, Return to the Moon, and on to Mars, 2021, ISBN-979-8490532361.

James Webb Space Telescope. A New Era in Astronomy, 2021, ISBN-979-8773857969.